a Pathway to God

a Pathway to God

GENE MERZ, SJ

PHOTOGRAPHS BY DON DOLL, SJ

Pilgrimage and Labor. The congregation invites the entire Society to read and pray over this updating of our law and orientation of our mission for today. One way of doing this would be in the light of the Ignatian images of pilgrimage and labor.

Just as the pilgrim Ignatius found that 'God treated him…as a schoolmaster treats a child whom he is teaching,' so Ignatius, as general and master of the spiritual life, continued his journey into the more profound discovery of God. The pilgrim search of Ignatius united him to Christ, led him to choose poverty with Christ poor, and to enter more deeply into the mystery of Christ's passion and resurrection. Out of his incessant search for God's presence and will, Ignatius developed a way of proceeding. This way of proceeding is found in the pilgrimage of the Spiritual Exercises from sinner beloved and forgiven to disciple called to labor in the vineyard and to suffer with Christ; it is in the pilgrimage of the Constitutions from the first inquiry about the Society in the **General Examen** *to the mature acceptance of responsibility for the Society in* **Parts V-X;** *it is in the personal examen of his own life where each Jesuit finds his own pathway to God.…Like that of Ignatius, our way of proceeding is both a pilgrimage and a labor in Christ: in his compassion, in his ceaseless desire to bring men and women to the Father's reconciliation and the Spirit's love, and in his committed care for the poor, the marginalized, and the abandoned.*

—GC 34, Decree 1: United with Christ on Mission #4-5

Foreword

In my address to our gathering at Province Days last June I spoke of our intention to make a province retreat together, in the manner of the 19th Annotation of the Exercises. I said then that we were trying to put together materials so that we have the *Constitutions and Complementary Norms*, the Spiritual Exercises, and coordination with the liturgical seasons.

Father Gene Merz undertook the development of this book to give us a framework for our prayer and sharing. I am very grateful for his work; he has given us an excellent guide. It does indeed offer us a way of using the various documents and the liturgy through the course of 27 weeks as a basis of our prayer.

I also emphasized in my address that I am looking for communities to do this together. Superiors with their communities will develop the program so that we will be sharing the fruit of our prayer, talking about what the Constitutions mean to us, bringing to that sharing our personal experience in prayer and in the mission we have been given. It is important that we share this, for we are one apostolic body, with a common mission, however diverse may be our individual assignments.

The Lord will surely bless our efforts in this retreat together and lead us into the conversion and freedom that will ready us for our review of ministries.

D. Edward Mathie, SJ
PROVINCIAL, WISCONSIN

A Blessing

CURIA PRÆPOSITI GENERALIS
SOCIETATIS IESU
ROMA - Borgo S. Spirito, 5

November 14, 1997
Feast of St. Joseph Pignatelli

To the Members of the Wisconsin Province:

Dear Brothers in Christ, P.C.

With the coming feast of Christ the King, you will begin a shared experience of reflection and prayer on the Decrees of the 34th General Congregation and the *Constitutions and Complementary Norms*, integrating them with the Spiritual Exercises in its 19th Annotation format, the Liturgical Year, and Scripture. This is a wonderful opportunity, and I write to wish you all the best and to assure you that my prayers will accompany you in this journey.

While the preparations for and the actual experience of GC 34 were not always an easy matter, filled with evident light in the pursuit of clear directions, the Congregation, in retrospect, can be called nothing less than a miracle of the Holy Spirit. You have all read the documents and can attest to the richness of grace that has been given to us in them. May this same Spirit, who has called us to this moment in our history, be with us as we assimilate these graces and make them a living dimension of all we are and do, in the many cultural and historical contexts in which we live and work!

This is my prayer for you, the Wisconsin Province, as you undertake the coming adventurous months of prayer, assimilation, and discernment.

Sincerely in Christ,

Peter-Hans Kolvenbach, SJ
GENERAL SUPERIOR OF THE SOCIETY OF JESUS

Introduction

The image of Ignatius the Pilgrim, "leaning into the wind," offers us an apt icon as we begin our retreat. Poets, mystics and philosophers have mused about life as a journey. The people of God in biblical tradition are depicted as on a journey to the New Jerusalem. After the Resurrection, two disciples traveling to Emmaus, found their eyes opened and their hearts afire as they recognized the Lord Jesus with them on their journey. It is not surprising then to find in the writings of Ignatius various allusions to journey. In his *Autobiography,* Ignatius called himself "the Pilgrim."

Another journey image is found in the *Formula of Institute of the Society of Jesus*: "a pathway to God." Dear to the heart of Ignatius and the early companions, "a pathway to God" refers to the *Constitutions of the Society of Jesus* which Ignatius knew would be for him, and all of us, a guiding path on our journey to God.

So, as "friends in the Lord" on a pilgrimage through this world in need, we turn to the prayer experience of the *Spiritual Exercises*, a spiritual journey, which profoundly shaped the life of Ignatius.

> *Out of his incessant search for God's presence and will, Ignatius developed a way of proceeding. This way of proceeding is found in the pilgrimage of the Spiritual Exercises from sinner beloved and forgiven to disciple called to labor in the vineyard and to suffer with Christ; it is in the pilgrimage of the Constitutions from the first inquiry about the Society in the General Examen to the mature acceptance of responsibility for the Society in Parts V-X; it is in the personal examen of his own life where each Jesuit finds his own pathway to God.* —GC34, Decree 1: United with Christ on Mission #5

My hope in designing this retreat has been that we would experience individually and together the God who loves us and frees us for mission.

To this end, the retreat format, based on the rhythm and dynamic of the *Spiritual Exercises* includes an opportunity to reflect upon and appropriate the *Constitutions and Complementary Norms* as well as several decrees from GC 34. Further supports to our reflection and prayer will be: *Our Way of Proceeding*, by William A. Barry, SJ; the photography of Don Doll, SJ; *Draw Me Into Your Friendship, The Spiritual Exercises, A Literal Translation and a Contemporary Reading* by David L. Fleming, SJ; and the rhythm of the liturgical year.

A few words are appropriate about the process and our basic dispositions as we enter into this retreat. The retreat design is simple, flexible and respectful of each person's present manner of prayer. The structure for each week contains: a focus which offers a theme to orient the week's prayer and conversation; the grace to be sought during the week; a series of texts for prayer and reflection; citations for liturgical feasts; finally, a series of questions for personal reflection and conversation. I designed the retreat in this manner to provide a way for us, as Ignatius suggests, to come reverently before God in prayer, open and attentive to God's word and movements within us. Hopefully, this format will enable us to remain where our minds and hearts are being held. Since the retreat is extended over a period of twenty-seven weeks, you may want to consider the suggestion of Ignatius to briefly record the grace received each week as a gift for future reflection. I hope we will find the retreat to be a prayerful experience, not a project to accomplish!

This retreat presents a wonderful opportunity to explore and discuss in a prayerful context the richness of our *Constitutions and Complementary Norms*—our "pathway to God." Selected key texts are presented for your reading and prayer. You will notice that this text honors the basic divisions in William Barry's book, *Our Way of Proceeding*. Some may wish to use his book as spiritual reading or as an Office reading during the retreat. Throughout the retreat, I would hope individuals and communities would be free to make necessary adaptations "according to the circumstances of persons, places and times." Pray as you are moved by the Lord!

With Ignatius the Pilgrim, we, too, are moving into our future as Servants of Christ's Mission. The powerful photographs of Don Doll, SJ may reveal to us the face of God in the faces of God's people. They are a visual reminder of the desire and the commitment to the service of faith and the promotion of justice. Allow the cries of the poor and the images of God's people to hold you in prayer. Do we, with childlike hope and trust, dare to venture into the uncertainty and darkness of an unknown future, empowered by faith in a God who first loved us? I look forward to praying with you and for you as together we make this journey on our "pathway to God."

Eugene F. Merz, SJ
September 4, 1997

Week 1

November 23-29, 1997

For Prayer

Spiritual Exercises: #5, 91-97
Complementary Norms: #4

Celebrations

Nov. 23: Christ the King
Nov. 26: St. John Berchmans, SJ
Nov. 27: Thanksgiving

For Reflection

Formulas of the Institute
cf. Constitutions and
Complementary Norms:
   p. 3-14
Constitutions:
   Forward: pp. vii-x
   Preface: P. H. Kolvenbach, SJ: xi-xiv
   Preface to 1st Edition: xv-xx
Complementary Norms:
   #1-23, pp. 57, 59, 61-69

Whoever desires to serve…beneath the banner of the cross in our Society,…should…take care, as long as he lives, first of all to keep before his eyes God and then the nature of this Institute which is, so to speak, **a pathway to God***; and then let him strive with all his effort to achieve this end set before him by God…*
                    —Formula #1

Focus

Openness: to the deepening of the grace of my vocation; to the gifts God desires to give me in this retreat.

Grace

I beg for an interior knowledge of the nature of my Jesuit vocation and our way of proceeding as a **"pathway to God."**

Questions

As I prayerfully ponder the texts and readings, where do I experience confirmation, consolation, resistance and desolation? What captures my attention in either a positive or negative way?

When I consider God's goodness to me, especially key moments, events and persons in my life, for which gifts am I most grateful? How does my gratitude move me to generous sharing of these gifts?

What is the quality of my openness to God's Spirit working in my life and in the lives of other people? How have I found God "laboring" in my ministry and in the people of God?

Our Way of Proceeding
Week I

Week 2

November 30-December 6, 1997

For Prayer

Spiritual Exercises:
　　#23, The Principle and Foundation
General Examen:
　　[3], [51], [93], [101], [134]

Celebrations

Nov. 30: First Sunday of Advent
Dec. 1: St. Edmund Campion, SJ
Dec. 3: St. Francis Xavier, SJ

For Reflection

Constitutions: # [1-133], pp.23-54
　　*The First and General Examen which
　　should be proposed to all who ask for
　　Admission into the Society of Jesus*
Preamble to Constitutions.
　　[134-137], pp. 56-58

Our Way of Proceeding
Week II

The end of this Society is to devote itself with God's grace not only to the salvation and perfection of the members' own souls, but also with that same grace to labor strenuously in giving aid toward the salvation and perfection of the souls of their neighbors. —General Examen #[3]

Therefore, those who will come to us should, before they take this burden upon their shoulders, ponder long and seriously, as the Lord has counseled ...whether the Holy Spirit who moves them is offering them so much grace that with his aid they have hope of bearing the weight of this vocation. —Formula #4, pp. 7-8.

Focus

My Jesuit Identity…in freedom…before God

Grace

I beg for a profound appreciation and gratitude for being called to the Company of Jesus and for the grace to be faithful to my Jesuit identity.

Questions

How do I experience myself as a Jesuit before God at this moment in my life?

What is my experience as I prayerfully ponder the *Formula* and *General Examen* as the "Principle and Foundation" of my Jesuit life?

Week 3

For Prayer

Spiritual Exercises: #45-48, 53-54, 55-61, 63
   Psalm 139
Constitutions: [288]
Complementary Norms: #45

Celebrations

Dec. 8: Immaculate Conception
   Gen. 3:9-15,20; Eph. 1:3-6,11-12;
   Lk. 1:26-38

For Reflection

Constitutions:
   Part I, The Admission to Probation.
   [138]-[203], pp. 70-90
Complementary Norms:
   #24-32, pp. 71-87
Constitutions:
   Part II, The Dismissal of those who
   were admitted but did not prove themselves fit. [204]-[242], pp. 92-107
Complementary Norms:
   #34-38, pp. 93,97,101,105
Constitutions:
   Part III, The Preservation and Progress
   of those who remain in probation.
   [243]-[306], pp. 108-128
Complementary Norms:
   #39-58, pp. 109-11

Our Way of Proceeding
Week III

Yahweh, you examine me and know me, you know when I sit, when I rise, you understand my thoughts from afar.…Where shall I go to escape your spirit? Where shall I flee from your presence?…If I speed away on the wings of the dawn, if I dwell beyond the ocean, even there your hand will be guiding me, your right hand holding me fast.… You created my inmost self, knit me together in my mother's womb. For so many marvels I thank you; a wonder am I, and all your works are wonders. God, examine me and know my heart, test me and know my concerns. Make sure that I am not on my way to ruin, and guide me on the road of eternity.
—Psalm 139:1-2,7,9-10,13-14,23-24

Focus

The Reality of Sin, the Mystery of Vocation; Formation for Mission

Grace

I beg for the grace "to be a Jesuit…(who knows)…that one is a sinner, yet called to be a companion of Jesus as Ignatius was."
—GC 32, Decree 2: Jesuits Today #11

Questions

At this stage of my life, what are the patterns of my sinfulness? What is my basic sin? What are my fears? Do these fears prevent me from responding freely to God?

What in my formation do I need to retrieve and re-appropriate?
Regardless of age, infirmity or ministry, how do I re-appropriate basic Jesuit values so as to envision a future?

Mary was called, conceived without sin and was chosen to be the Mother of Jesus; I was called, "a sinner yet loved" and chosen to be a Companion of Jesus. God carefully chose and formed Mary to be the Mother of Jesus; the Society carefully chooses and forms us to be Companions of Jesus.
What do I experience when I prayerfully ponder the gift of my vocation?

"Young men dream dreams and old men see visions." What is helping me surrender broken dreams to God and be open to new visions and realities in a constantly changing world?

Week 4

December 14-20, 1997

For Prayer

Spiritual Exercises: #53
Constitutions: [307]-[308]
Complementary Norms:
  #59-60, 65, 81, 82

Celebrations

Dec. 14: Gaudete Sunday
  Zeph. 3:14-18; Phil. 4:4-7
  Lk. 3:10-18

For Reflection

Constitutions:
  Part IV, The learning and other means
  of helping their neighbor that are to be
  imparted to those who are retained in
  the Society.
  Ch. 1-7, [307]-[309], pp. 130-166
Complementary Norms:
  #59-112, pp. 131-173

Our Way of Proceeding
Week IV

Colloquy: I put myself before Jesus Christ our Lord, present before me on the cross. I talk to him about how he creates because he loves and then he becomes man out of love, so emptying himself as to pass from eternal life to death here in time, even death on a cross, that by his obedience of love given to his Father he might die for my sins. I look to myself and ask—just letting the question penetrate my being: In the past, what response have I made to Christ? How do I respond to Christ now? What response should I make to Christ? As I look upon Jesus as he hangs upon the cross, I ponder whatever God may bring to my attention. I close with an Our Father.   —Spiritual Exercise: #53

Focus

The Reality of **God's mercy**;
The **Advent of the Word** Made Flesh—Emmanuel;
Excellence in learning and solid **formation** are essential for the apostolic mission of the Society of Jesus.

Grace

I beg for the grace to forgive as I wish to be forgiven.

Questions

What prevents me from trusting more in God's mercy? When and how do I celebrate the sacrament of reconciliation? Is there anyone I have not forgiven?

Who and what do I find most difficult to accept in my life? Do I desire to surrender this to God? What further growth is God asking of me this day?

> *Our studies should foster and stimulate those very qualities that today are often choked off by our contemporary style of living and thinking: a spirit of reflection and an awareness of deeper, transcendent values.   —Complementary Norms: #82*

When and where do I find moments of quality reflection in the rhythm and patterns of my life? How open am I to the Advent of God in the human circumstances of my life?

Week 5

For Prayer

Spiritual Exercises: #101-126

The Word was made flesh and dwelt among us.
The Nativity of our Lord Jesus Christ.

Celebrations

Dec. 25: The Nativity of Our Lord Jesus Christ
Midnight
Is. 9:1-6, Ti. 2:11-14, Lk. 2:1-14
Dawn
Is. 62:11-12, Ti. 3:4-7, Lk. 2:15-20
Day
Is. 52:7-10, Heb. 1:1-6, Jn. 1:1-18
Dec. 26: St. Stephen, Martyr
Dec. 27: St. John, Apostle

For Reflection

No reading this week…ponder the mystery.

I try to enter into the vision of God—the mystery of divinity shared by three divine persons—looking upon our world: men and women being born and being laid to rest, some getting married and others getting divorced, the old and the young, the rich and the poor, the happy and the sad, so many people aimless, despairing, hateful, and killing, so many undernourished, sick and dying, so many struggling with life and blind to any meaning. With God, I can hear people laughing and crying, some shouting and screaming, some praying, others cursing….hear the Divine Persons saying 'Let us work the redemption of the whole human race; let us respond to the groaning of all creation.'
—Spiritual Exercises: #101-126

Focus

The Mysteries of The Incarnation and the Nativity

Grace

I ask for the grace to know Jesus intimately, to love him more intensely, and so to follow him more closely.
—Spiritual Exercises: #104

Questions

What does the birth and humanity of Jesus mean in my life?

The Father chose that Jesus be born in poverty. How is Jesus' poverty reflected in my choices and value system as a companion of Jesus?

What is my response to his question, "Who do you say I am?"

Week 6

For Prayer

Spiritual Exercises: #109, 132-135
Complementary Norms: #111
Constitutions: [414]
Complementary Norms: #106, 110

Celebrations

Dec. 28: Holy Family Sunday
World Day of Peace
Si. 3:2-6, Col. 3:12-17, Lk. 2:41-52
Jan. 1: Mary, Mother of God;
Giving the Name Jesus
Nu. 6:22-27, Gal. 4:4-7, Lk. 2:16-21

For Reflection

Constitutions:
Part IV cont., Ch. 8-17, pp. 166-190
GC 34, Decree 16:
The Intellectual Dimension
of Jesuit Ministries

Our Way of Proceeding
Week V

…Ridding themselves of nationalism and every other form of particularism, they will acquire the universality of mind and the openness toward different forms of cultures, diverse civilizations, and differing mentalities that our apostolic vocation demands.

—Complementary Norms: #111

Focus

The Hidden Life and The Apostolate of Studies in Jesuit Formation

Grace

As I recall important formative experiences in my own Jesuit life, I beg for the grace to deepen my gratitude for the people who have shaped my life and ministry and to appreciate "the way God wants to form us for his purposes." I pray also for the grace to understand obedience and authority according to the mind and heart of Ignatius.

Questions

As we celebrate Holy Family Sunday, what surfaces within me when I remember my own family of origin?

What are my feelings and thoughts when I experience the hiddenness of Jesus in my personal and Jesuit community life? What gifts do I bring to my community? Where do we as a Jesuit community need to grow?

> *The intellectual dimension of every apostolic work also supposes that each Jesuit knows how to be active in companionship with others.*
> —GC 34, Decree 16: The Intellectual Dimension of Jesuit Ministries #398

Where do I need to grow in working with others? What do I do to guard against individualism?

> *For evangelization to be effective, accuracy in knowledge, respect for the other in intercultural dialogue, and critical analysis are all imperative.*
> —GC 34, Decree 16: The Intellectual Dimension of Jesuit Ministries #396

What were my reflections as I read this decree which stresses the importance of the intellectual dimension for all of our ministries?

Week 7

For Prayer

GC 34, Decree 4: Our Mission and Culture
#76, 77, 88, 97, 101

Celebrations

Epiphany Sunday
Is. 60:1-6; Eph. 3:2-3,5-6; Mt. 2:1-12

For Reflection

GC 34, Decree 4: Our Mission and Culture

The Christian message is to be open to all cultures, bound to no single culture and made accessible to every human person through a process of inculturation, by which the Gospel introduces something new into the culture, and the culture brings something new to the richness of the Gospel….Through inculturation the Church makes the Gospel incarnate in different cultures and at the same time introduces people, together with their cultures, into her own community. She transmits to them her own values, at the same time taking the good elements that already exist in them and renewing them from within.
—GC 34, Decree 4: Our Mission and Culture #76

Evangelization is not possible without inculturation. Inculturation is the existential dialogue between a living people and the living Gospel.
—GC 34, Decree 4: Our Mission and Culture #77

Focus

Epiphany of our Lord Jesus Christ
New Manifestations in Mission

Grace

I beg to be open to receive the gifts God desires for me and the Society through this document which speaks of God present and active in diverse cultures and traditions.

Questions

Where and how do I experience the Epiphany of our Lord in the passion of His people?

What is the fundamental message in this document on Mission and Culture? Where do I personally find consolation and challenge in this document?

What has been my most significant, enriching and challenging cultural experience?

What are some further specific ways this document can be implemented in my ministry?

Week 8

For Prayer

Spiritual Exercises: #273 (Mt. 3:13-17)
Constitutions: [516], [542]
Complementary Norms: #120, 121, 125

Celebrations

The Baptism of the Lord
    Is. 42:1-4,6-7; Acts 10:34-38;
    Lk. 3:15-16,21-22

For Reflection

Constitutions:
    Part V, Admission or Incorporation into
    the Society. [510]-[546], pp. 192-212
Complementary Norms:
    #113-142, pp. 193-213

Our Way of Proceeding
Week VI

'You are my Son, the Beloved; my favor rests on you.'   —Mk 1:11

Focus

Identity
    The **Baptism of the Lord**: Confirms the identity of Jesus.
    The **Vows**: Shape the identity of Jesuits.

Grace

I beg for the grace to be faithful to my identity as a Christian and as a vowed Jesuit. I also beg to be open to the ongoing conversion process which these commitments entail.

Questions

How has my appreciation for the significance of the Sacrament of Baptism grown?

How have each of the vows revealed to me my basic Jesuit identity before God? What specifically has helped me in my struggle to live these vows faithfully?

In the past, the reality of grades was a painful issue in the Society. As I reflect on my lived Jesuit experience, where have I found more peace with the Society's way of proceeding in this matter?

Ignatius saw the Superior General as "holding the place of God." What has been my experience of obedience and superiors in the Society? In the midst of both struggle and calm, how has my trust in God deepened?

Week 9

For Prayer

Spiritual Exercises: #274
    The Temptations of Jesus
    Lk. 4:1-13, Mt. 4:1-11, Heb. 4:14-16
Constitutions:
    Part VI, The Personal Life of Those
    Already Admitted and Incorporated into
    the Body of the Society. [547]
Complementary Norms:
    Sections 1 and 2: #143-148. Chastity

Celebrations

Jan. 18: Ecumenical Sunday;
    Christian Unity Week
Complementary Norms: #26

For Reflection

Constitutions: [547], pp. 220-222
Complementary Norms: #143-148,
    pp. 215-219

Our Way of Proceeding
Week VII

…for it is not as if we had a high priest who was incapable of feeling our weaknesses with us; but we have one who has been tempted in every way that we are, though he is without sin. Let us be confident, then, in approaching the throne of grace, that we shall have mercy from him and find grace when we are in need of help.
                                                                      —Heb. 4:14-16

Faith which does justice is necessarily committed to ecumenical dialogue and cooperation. Ecumenism is not only a specific work for which some Jesuits must be trained and missioned, it is a new way of living as a Christian. It seeks, namely, what unites rather than what divides; it seeks understanding rather than confrontation, it seeks to know, understand, and love others as they wish to be known and understood, with full respect for their distinctiveness, through dialogue of truth, justice, and love.
                                                    —Complementary Norms: #268

Focus

Fidelity to Identity: The Temptations of Jesus, Efforts at Ecumenism, Chastity

Grace

In the midst of struggle and temptation, I beg for the grace to be faithful to my identity, strengthened and consoled by the humanity of Jesus.

Questions

Since the vows shape my identity as a Jesuit, how has chastity helped me to grow in my Jesuit identity? In my effort to be chaste, am I more loving?

The vows are pronounced in and received by the Society. How has the Jesuit community helped me to live chastely?

In what way has living the vow of chastity freed me for mission? Where am I not free? What do I need to do to be more free for mission?

At La Storta, the Father promised "to be present" to Ignatius. The charism of the founder is shared with the members. How have I experienced God "to be present" to me in my effort to live the vow of chastity?

Week 10

January 25-31, 1998

For Prayer

Spiritual Exercises: #275
    Phil. 3:7-11, Jn. 1:35-51, Mt. 4:18-22,
    Lk. 5:1-11
Constitutions:
    Part VI, cont., ch. 1 [547], [551]
Complementary Norms:
    Section 3, #149, 150, 151

Celebrations

Jan. 25: Conversion of St. Paul
    Neh. 8: 2-6, 8-10, 1 Cor. 12: 12-30
    Lk. 1:1-4, 14-21

For Reflection

Constitutions:
    Part VI, [547]-[552], pp. 220-224
Complementary Norms:
    #143, 149-156, pp. 215-227

Our Way of Proceeding
Week VIII

…because of Christ, I have come to consider all these advantages that I had as disadvantages. Not only that, but I believe nothing can happen that will outweigh the supreme advantage of knowing Christ Jesus my Lord. For him I have accepted the loss of everything, and I look on everything as so much rubbish if only I can have Christ and be given a place in him. I am no longer trying for perfection by my own efforts, the perfection that comes from the law, but I want only the perfection that comes through faith in Christ, and is from God and based on faith. All I want is to know Christ and the power of his resurrection and to share his sufferings by reproducing the pattern of his death.

—Phil. 3:7-11

Focus
Obedience

Grace
I beg for the grace to re-commit myself to the call of Jesus to obedient discipleship.

Questions

As I reflect on the conversion of St. Paul, what areas in my life need a "conversion of heart?" How and where do I find in my life of obedience, the joy of Jesus in doing the Father's will?

Since the vows shape my identity as a Jesuit, how has obedience helped me to grow in my Jesuit identity?

Vows are pronounced in and received by the Society. How has the Jesuit community helped me to live obediently?

In what way has living the vow of obedience freed me for mission? Where am I not free? What do I need to do to be more free for mission?

At La Storta, the Father promised "to be present" to Ignatius. The charism of the founder is shared with the members. How have I experienced God "to be present" to me in my effort to live the vow of obedience?

Week 11

February 1-7, 1998

For Prayer

Spiritual Exercises: #136-148
   The Two Standards
Constitutions:
   Part VI cont., [553]
Complementary Norms:
   #157-165, 176-180, 199-200, 210
Examen: #44

Celebrations

Feb. 2: Presentation of the Lord
Feb. 4: St. John de Brito, SJ
Feb. 6: St. Paul Miki, SJ

For Reflection

Constitutions:
   [553]-[581], pp. 226-238
Complementary Norms:
   #157-222 pp. 227-253

Our Way of Proceeding
Week IX

…to abhor completely…all that the world loves and embraces, to accept and desire with all (our) strength whatever Christ…loved and embraced. For, as men of the world…love and…seek honors, distinctions, and the reputation of a great name…so (we) who…are serious about following Christ…love and…desire the very opposite…out of love and reverence for him:…to such an extent, that if it could be done without offense to his Divine Majesty, or sin on the part of (our) neighbor, (we)…wish to suffer abuse, injustice, false accusations, and to be considered and treated as fools (without, however, giving occasion for such treatment), (our) whole desire being to resemble, and in some way imitate…Jesus Christ,…(who) gave us an example to…seek…to imitate and follow him, seeing he is the true Way which leads to life.
        —Examen #44

Focus
The Two Standards and Jesuit Poverty

Grace
I beg for the grace to desire to live the standard of Christ.

Questions
Since the vows shape my identity as a Jesuit, how has the vow of poverty helped me to grow in my Jesuit identity?

The vows are pronounced in and received by the Society. How has the Jesuit community helped me to live simply and with frugality?

In what way has living the vow of poverty freed me for mission? Where am I not free? What do I need to do to be more free for mission?

At La Storta, the Father promised "to be present" to Ignatius. The charism of the founder is shared with the members. How have I experienced God "to be present" to me in my effort to live the vow of poverty?

Week 12

February 8-14, 1998

For Prayer
Spiritual Exercises: #149-156
Complementary Norms: #4, p. 61
GC 34, Decree 3:
   Our Mission and Justice #51, 50

Celebrations
5th Sunday of the year
   Is. 6:1-8, 1 Cor. 15:1-11, Jn. 5:1-11

For Reflection
GC 34, Decree 3:
   Our Mission and Justice

We also acknowledge our failures on the journey. The promotion of justice has sometimes been separated from its well-spring of faith. Dogmatism or ideology sometimes led us to treat each other more as adversaries than as companions. We can be timid in challenging ourselves and our institutional apostolates with the fullness of our mission of faith seeking justice.
       —GC 34, Decree 3: Our Mission and Justice #51

In response to the Second Vatican Council, we, the Society of Jesus, set out on a journey of faith as we committed ourselves to the promotion of justice as an integral part of our mission.
       —GC 34, Decree 3: Our Mission and Justice #50

Focus
The Three Types of Persons: A Faith that **does** Justice

Grace
We beg for the grace "as servants of Christ's mission,…(to open) our hearts and our very lives to 'the joys and hopes, the griefs and the anxieties of the men and women of this age, especially those who are poor or in any way afflicted.'"   —GC 34, Decree 3: Our Mission and Justice #50

Questions
What personal challenge do I find in this decree on "Our Mission and Justice?" What can I do with the resistance and fear within me when I try to live this call to faith which does justice?

In my ministry and personal attitudes, how have I grown in my efforts to be more personally committed to the promotion of justice as an integral part of our mission? As I reflect on this decree, what surfaces in my consciousness as to how I can further integrate both faith and justice into my ministry?

What holds me back in these efforts? What grace do I need to be able to move more freely toward embracing this invitation? What "type of person" am I when I consider the demands of justice?

Week 13

For Prayer

Spiritual Exercises: #278
    Mt.5:1-48 Sermon, Beatitudes
Spiritual Exercises: #164-168
    Three Modes of Humility
Spiritual Exercises: #167
Constitutions:
    Part VI, [595-596], [602]
Complementary Norms:
    #223-227, 229, 240, 244

Celebrations

Feb. 15: St. Claude de la Colombiere, SJ

For Reflection

Constitutions: Part VI, Section 5,
    [582]-[602] pp. 254-268
Complementary Norms: #223-244
    pp. 255-267

Our Way of Proceeding
Week X

I so much want the truth of Christ's life to be fully the truth of my own that I find myself, moved by grace, with a love and a desire for poverty in order to be with the poor Christ; a love and a desire for insults in order to be closer to Christ in his own rejection by people; a love and a desire to be considered worthless and a fool for Christ, rather than to be esteemed as wise and prudent, according to the standards of the world. By grace, I find myself so moved to follow Jesus Christ in the most intimate union possible, that his experiences are reflected in my own. In that, I find my delight.
                                    —Spiritual Exercises: #167

Focus

Three Modes of Humility: Sermon on the Mount and the Beatitudes

Grace

I should beg our Lord to choose me for the gift of this third kind of humility in order that I may find my own life more patterned according to Jesus, my God and Lord—always, of course, if this is to be for the greater praise and service of God.   —Spiritual Exercises: #168

Questions

The integration of prayer and action marked the life of Ignatius. "Prayer...makes increasingly evident in us the action and presence of God, whereby we are enabled to seek, love, and serve him in all things." At this moment in my life, how do I assess the integration of prayer with my ministry?

What is the quality of my prayer? What forms of prayer have been helpful in the past? Have any desires surfaced within me as I ponder my prayer relationship with God?

In what areas do I feel called to change my patterns of Jesuit living?

Week 14

February 22-28, 1998

For Prayer

Spiritual Exercises: #285
  Jn. 11:1-46
Constitutions: Part VII,
  The Relations to Their Neighbor of
  Those Already Incorporated into the
  Society When They are Dispersed into the
  Vineyard of Christ our Lord. [621-623]
Complementary Norms:
  #245-249, 252-257

Celebrations

Feb. 25: Ash Wednesday
  Jl. 2:12-18; 2 Cor. 5:20-6:2;
  Mt. 6:1-6, 16-18

For Reflection

Constitutions: Part VII,
  ch. 1, 2, [603-632] pp. 276-292
Complementary Norms:
  The Mission and Ministries of the Society,
  #245-262, pp. 271-289

Our Way of Proceeding
Week XI

…the contemporary mission of the Society is the service of faith and the promotion in society of that justice of the Gospel that is the embodiment of God's love and saving mercy. In this mission, its aim (the service of faith) and its integrating principle (faith directed toward the justice of the Kingdom) are dynamically related to the inculturated proclamation of the Gospel and to dialogue with other religious traditions as integral dimensions of evangelization.

—Complementary Norms #245

Focus

Raising of Lazarus
The Contemporary Mission of the Society of Jesus

Grace

The service and love of God and of neighbor should shine out in my dedication. At this time, I should deepen the attitudes and search out the ways which will better enable me to live the Christ-life in my own surroundings and environment. For my progress in living out my life in Christ will be in proportion to the surrender of my own self-love and of my own will and interests.

—Spiritual Exercises: #189

Questions

What is my personal reaction to the Society's mission as stated above in Complementary Norm #245?

Complementary Norm #246 lists eight conditions for carrying out our mission.
What are my thoughts and feelings as I pray over these conditions?

What new life is the Lord calling forth in my life?

Week 15

March 1-7, 1998

For Prayer

Spiritual Exercises: #283
    Multiplication of the loaves and fish
    Mt. 14:13-21, Jn. 6:1-15
Constitutions:
    Part VII, [624-626]
Complementary Norms:
    265-266, 268
Eph. 3:14-21

Celebrations

First Sunday of Lent
    Dt. 26:4-10, Rom. 10:8-13, Lk. 4:1-13

For Reflection

Constitutions:
    Part VII, [624-635], pp. 288-294
Complementary Norms: #259-276,
    pp. 287-302

Our Way of Proceeding
Week XII

This, then is what I pray, kneeling before the Father, from whom every family, whether spiritual or natural, takes its name: Out of his infinite glory, may he give you the power through his Spirit for your hidden self to grow strong, so that Christ may live in your hearts through faith, and then, planted in love and built on love, you will with all the saints have strength to grasp the breadth and the length, the height and the depth, until, knowing the love of Christ, which is beyond all knowledge, you are filled with the utter fullness of God. Glory be to him whose power, working in us, can do infinitely more than we can ask or imagine; glory be to him from generation to generation in the Church and in Christ Jesus for ever and ever. Amen.   —Eph. 3:14-21

Focus

Ministries of the Society of Jesus: a share in God's generosity

Grace

I pray for the grace to trust that the power of God will work in my poverty to feed the lives of God's people.

Questions

Part VII lists the Ministries by which the Society fulfills its Mission: This week * consider these four areas: Missionary service, Inter-religious Dialogue, Ecumenical activity and Pastoral Services and Works. *(Five other ministries will be considered next week when the last section of Part VII is considered.)*

What is my reaction when I reflect on these ministries?

Where do I find hope, encouragement and challenge? Where do I experience fear or resistance?

Jesus fed the people with only a few loaves and fish. Am I comfortable in allowing the Lord to feed the people from my poverty? What do I do with the empty nets in my community life and ministry?

Week 16

For Prayer

Spiritual Exercises: #281
   Mt.10:1-16
Spiritual Exercises: #280
   Mt.14:22-33, Jn. 6:16-21
Constitutions:
   Part VII, Ch. 4, [636-638], [650]
Complementary Norms:
   #277-279, 288-289, 293-297, 298,
   305-306, 309

Celebrations

Second Week of Lent
   Gn. 15:5-12, 17-18; Phil 3:17-41;
   Lk. 9:28-36

For Reflection

Constitutions:
   Part VII, [636-654] pp. 294-298
Complementary Norms:
   #277-310 pp. 302-315

Our Way of Proceeding
Week XIII

The service of faith and the promotion of justice constitute one and the same mission of the Society. They cannot, therefore, be separated one from the other in our purpose, our action, our life; nor can they be considered simply as one ministry among others, but rather as that ministry whereby all our ministries are brought together in a unified whole.   —Complementary Norms: #4.2

Focus

Ministries of the Society of Jesus: a share in God's compassion

Grace

Persons who are of great heart and are set on fire with zeal to follow Jesus Christ, eternal King and Lord of all, will not only offer themselves entirely for such a mission, but will act against anything that would make their response less total.   —Spiritual Exercises: #97

Questions

Part VII concludes the list of the Ministries by which the Society fulfills its Mission: Educational apostolate, Intellectual apostolate, Social apostolate, Social communications, Interprovincial works and houses in Rome.

What is my reaction when I reflect on these ministries?

Where do I find hope, encouragement and challenge? Where do I experience fear or resistance?

One of the purposes of this retreat is to come to openness and freedom necessary for the crucial ministry decisions to be made in the near future. Am I growing in openness, freedom, trust, surrender and availability?

WE ARE ALL MADE IN GOD'S IMAGE

Week 17

For Prayer

Spiritual Exercises: #282
    Lk. 7:36-50 Mary Magdalen
    Lk. 15:11-32 Prodigal Son
GC 34, Decree 14:
    #362, 364, 368, 369, 372

Celebrations

March 19: Joseph, Husband of Mary
    2 Sam. 7:4-5,12-14,16;
    Rom. 4:13,16-18,22; Mt. 1:16,18-21,24;
    or Lk. 2:41-51

For Reflection

GC 34, Decree 14:
    Jesuits and the Situation of Women
    in Church and Civil Society

The dominance of men in their relationship with women has found expression in…discrimination against women in educational opportunities, the disproportionate burden they are called upon to bear in family life, paying them a lesser wage for the same work, limiting their access to positions of influence when admitted to public life, and sadly but only too frequently, outright violence against women themselves….There is a 'feminization of poverty' and a distinctive 'feminine face of oppression.'…we are conscious of the damage to the People of God brought about in some cultures by the alienation of women who no longer feel at home in the Church and who are not able with integrity to transmit Catholic values to their families, friends, and colleagues….In response, we Jesuits first ask God for the grace of conversion. We have been part of a civil and ecclesial tradition that has offended against women. And, like many men, we have a tendency to convince ourselves that there is no problem. However unwittingly, we have often contributed to a form of clericalism…. By making this declaration we wish to react personally and collectively, and do what we can to change this regrettable situation….we invite all Jesuits to listen carefully and courageously to the experience of women. Many women feel that men simply do not listen to them. There is no substitute for such listening. More than anything else it will bring about change. —GC 34, Decree 14: #362, 364, 368, 369, 372

Focus

God's reverence for women

Grace

Colloquy: How can I respond to a God so good to me in himself and surrounding me with the goodness of his holy ones and all the gifts of his creation? All I can do is give thanks, wondering at his forgiving love, which continues to give me life up to this very moment. By his grace, I want to amend. —Spiritual Exercises: #61

Questions

What do I experience after prayerfully reading this decree about the situation of women in our world today?

Joseph stood before the mystery of Mary. He struggled to understand. What is my experience as a Jesuit and as a man as I struggle to understand the experience of women today as they, like us, move in faith to do God's will?

Joseph went down into Egypt; he lived in and experienced a different culture. What would it mean for me as a man if I were to imagine entering into our culture as it is experienced by women today?

Joseph accepted Mary and her total reality. What does it mean for me as a Jesuit to accept and support women today? In what ways do I affirm women and their gifts? Concretely, what practical steps am I taking to "align (myself) in solidarity with women"?

Joseph had dreams and visions. How free am I to dream or envision about the gifts of women in service of the Church both today and in the future?

Week 18

March 22-28, 1998

For Prayer

Spiritual Exercises: #284, 108
  Mt. 17:1-9
GC 34, Decree 5:
  Our Mission and Inter-Religious
  Dialogue #130

Celebrations

March 25:
  The Annunciation of the Virgin Mary
  Is. 7:10-14, 8:10; Heb. 10:4-10;
  Lk. 1:26-38

For Reflection

GC 34, Decree 5:
  Our Mission and Inter-Religious Dialogue

Dialogue is 'an activity with its own guiding principles, requirements, and dignity' and it should 'never be made a strategy to elicit conversions.' To be religious today is to be inter-religious in the sense that a positive relationship with believers of other faiths is a requirement in a world of religious pluralism.
—GC 34, Decree 5: Our Mission and Inter-Religious Dialogue #130

I let myself be totally present to the scene, hearing the nuances of the questions, seeing the expression in the face and eyes, watching the gestures and movements which tell us so much about a person.
—Spiritual Exercises: #108

Focus

Transfiguration of our Lord Jesus Christ
Jesuit Mission and Inter-Religious Dialogue

Grace

I pray for the grace to reverence the people whose way to God differs from my own.

Questions

What meaning and what opportunity does this rich ethnic, cultural and religious pluralism that characterizes God's world today have for our lives and for our mission of evangelization?

And how do we respond to the racism, cultural prejudice, religious fundamentalism and intolerance that mark so much of today's world?
—GC 34, Decree 5: Our Mission and Inter-Religious Dialogue #128

Am I personally willing and free "to move beyond prejudice and bias, be it historical, cultural, social, (sexual) or theological, and to cooperate wholeheartedly with all men and women of good will in promoting peace, justice, harmony, human rights and respect for all of God's creation"?

At the Annunciation, Mary said "yes" to the unknown. What is stirred in me at the thought of entering the unknown world of dialogue?

Mary listened to, heard, and responded in faith to God's word which radically changed her reality. Am I willing to surrender in faith to God's word of invitation to me?

Week 19

March 29-April 4, 1998

For Prayer

Spiritual Exercises: #190-199, 289
   Last Supper
   Jn. 13:1-17,26 Last Discourse
GC 34, Decree 6:
   Ministerial Priesthood and Jesuit Identity
   #168

Celebrations

5th Week of Lent
   Is. 43:16-21, Phil. 3:8-14, Jn. 8:1-11

For Reflection

GC 34, Decree 6:
   Ministerial Priesthood and Jesuit
   Identity
GC 34, Decree 7: The Jesuit Brother

Since the foundation of the Society, Jesuits have exercised their ministry most particularly where the needs are greatest, where there are not others to minister to these needs, and where the more universal good may be found. Jerome Nadal expressed this central aspect of our charism; "The society cares for those persons who are either totally neglected or inadequately attended to. This is the basic reason for the founding of the Society, this is its power, this is what makes it distinctive in the Church."

—GC 34, Decree 6: Ministerial Priesthood and Jesuit Identity #168

Focus

The Last Supper and Ministerial Priesthood

Grace

Jesus, may all that is you flow into me. May your body and blood be my food and drink. May your passion and death be my strength and life. Jesus, with you by my side enough has been given. May the shelter I seek be the shadow of your cross. Let me not run from the love which you offer, but hold me safe from the forces of evil. On each of my dyings shed your light and your love. Keep calling to me until that day comes, when, with your saints, I may praise you forever. Amen.

—The Prayer "Soul of Christ" translated by David L. Fleming, SJ

Questions

…we have been purified in the faith by which we live, and have grown in our understanding of our central mission. Our service, especially among the poor, has deepened our life of faith, both individually and as a body: our faith has become more paschal, more compassionate, more tender, more evangelical in its simplicity. —GC 34, Decree 15: Servants of Christ's Mission

In what ways do these characteristics describe my faith and priestly service?

What are the joys, sorrows, desires, pressures and gifts I experience in my ministry as a priest, brother or as one preparing for priesthood?

The reality of priesthood is under siege in our culture and society. How and where am I finding strength, courage and support for this radical commitment in faith?

Amid the stresses of his ministry to people, Jesus found a basic need for prayer and solitude. In what ways do I choose to be sustained, strengthened and renewed?

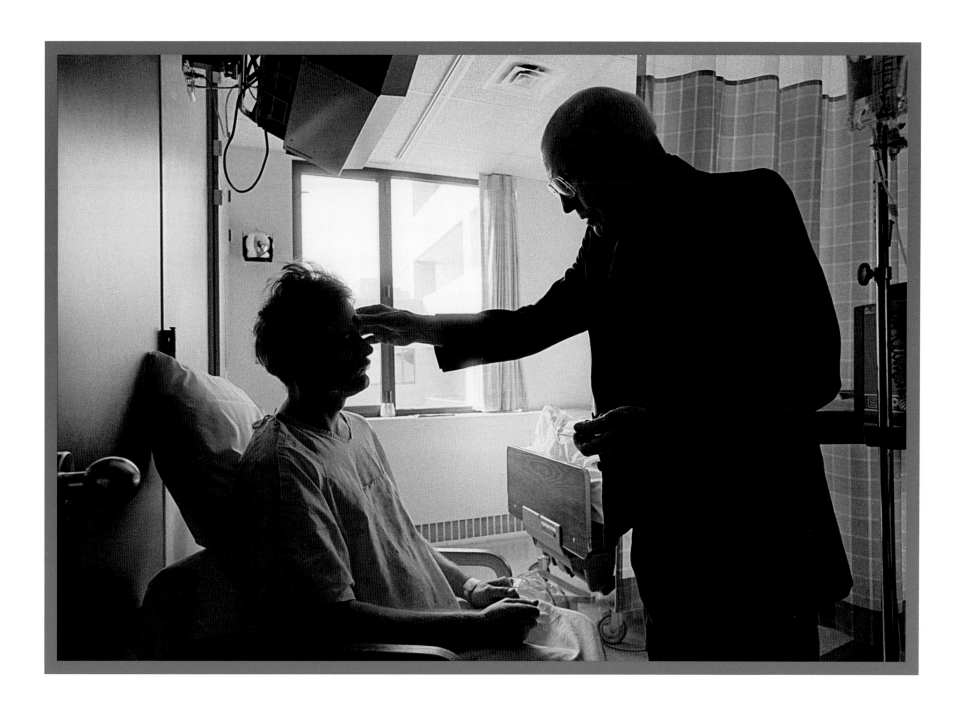

Week 20

April 5-11, 1998

For Prayer

Spiritual Exercises:
   #200-202, 290 Agony
   #291-295, From Garden to Pilate
   #296, Way of the Cross
   #297-298, Jesus dies

Celebrations

Palm Sunday
   Is. 50:4-7; Phil. 2:6-11; Lk. 22:14-23,56
Holy Thursday
   Ex. 12:1-8,11-14; 1 Cor. 11:23-26
   Jn. 13:1-15
Good Friday
   Is. 52:13, 53:12; Heb. 4:14-16, 5:7-9;
   Jn. 18:1,19:42
Holy Saturday
   Gen. 1:1-2:2; Gen. 22:1-18;
   Ex. 14:15, 15:1
   Is. 54:5-14; 55:1-11; Ba. 3:9-15, 32-4:4
   Ezec. 36:16-28; Rom. 6:3-11; Lk. 24:1-12

For Reflection

No reading this week…ponder the mystery

My people, what have I done to you? How have I offended you? Answer me.
— Reproaches of Good Friday

Focus
The Passion of our Lord Jesus

Grace
I continue to pray for the gift of being able to feel sorrow with Christ in sorrow, to be anguished with Christ's anguish, and even to experience tears and deep grief because of all the afflictions which Christ endures for me.   — Spiritual Exercises: #203

Questions
How am I embracing limitations, diminishment, aging and the approach of death?

Jesus embraced the powerlessness of the tomb. Do I patiently embrace the moments of emptiness and waiting in my life? What do I do with my present and past sufferings? In what way does the passion and death of Jesus shape my life?

How central is the Eucharist in my life as a Jesuit? In what specific ways do I feed and nourish God's people? In turn, how am I fed and nourished?

Ignatius begged to be "placed with Jesus," a prayer answered at La Storta.
Do I desire "to desire" that same grace?

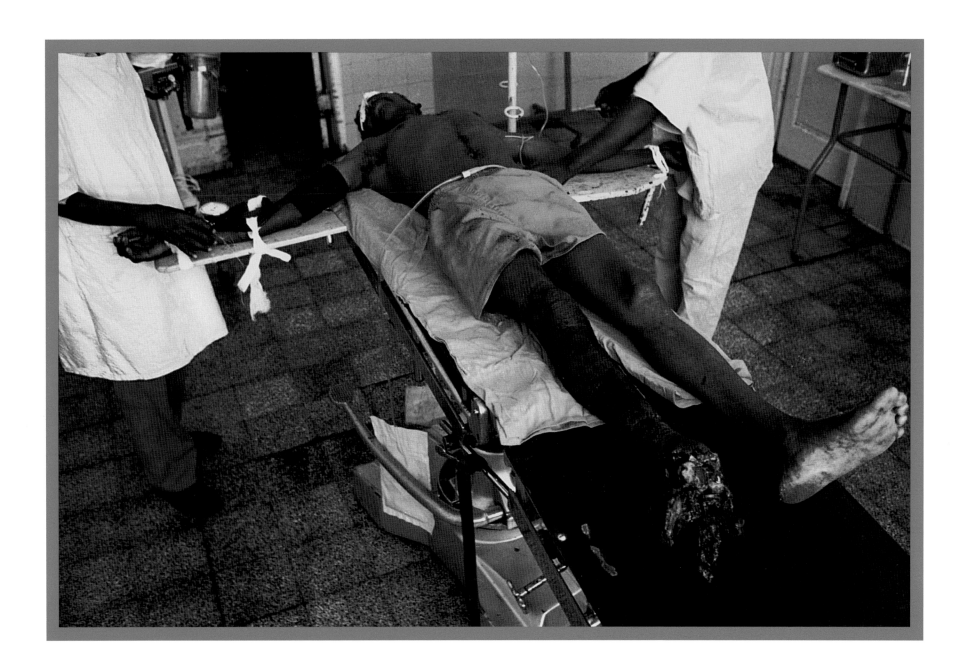

Week 21

For Prayer

Spiritual Exercises:

    #299, 218-225, Mary, Mother of God

    #300, Mary Magdalen

    Mk. 16:1-11

Celebrations

Easter Sunday

    Acts 10:34,37-43; Col. 3:1-4

    or 1 Cor. 5:6-8

    Jn. 20:1-9 or Lk. 24:1-12

For Reflection

GC 34, Decree 2:

    Servants of Christ's Mission

St. Ignatius was clear that, as the Society was not instituted by human means, so its ministries are preserved and fostered only by the all-powerful hand of Christ. Thus, as we receive our mission from Christ whatever fruitfulness it bears is entirely dependent on his grace. And it is the Risen Christ who calls and empowers us for his service under the banner of the Cross: the Risen Christ, far from being absent from the world's history, has begun a new presence to the world in the spirit. He is now present to all men and women and draws them into his Paschal Mystery. He continues to mediate God's work of bringing salvation, justice, and reconciliation to a world that is still broken by its sins.

        —GC 34, Decree 2: Servants of Christ's Mission #27-28

Focus

The Resurrection: Jesus Christ the Consoler

Grace

I beg for the gift of being able to enter into the joy and consolation of Jesus in the victory of his risen life.

        —Spiritual Exercises: #221

Questions

What stirs within me as I ponder the child in the doorway?

How have I experienced the presence of the Risen Lord to be the basic consolation of my being? In my Jesuit life, where have I been consoled by the Lord?

In the darkness, despair and pessimism of our culture, how am I a witness to radical hope in the person of Jesus?

> *…we have been purified in the faith by which we live and have grown in our understanding of our central mission. Our service, especially among the poor, has deepened our life of faith, both individually and as a body: our faith has become more paschal, more compassionate, more tender, more evangelical in its simplicity.*
>
>   —GC 34, Decree 2: Servants of Christ's Mission #15

Is this my experience both in ministry and in my Jesuit community?

Week 22

When community life flourishes, the whole religious life is sound; and unity and availability, universality, full personal dedication, and gospel freedom are also strengthened for the assistance of souls in every way.

—Complementary Norms: #316

For Prayer

Spiritual Exercises: #303, 236
    Lk. 24:13-35
Constitutions: Part VIII,
    Helps Toward Uniting the Dispersed
    Members with their Head and among
    Themselves. [655], [671]
Complementary Norms: #311, 314-316,
    319-320, 323

Celebrations

April 22: Mary, Mother of the Society of Jesus
April 25: St. Mark, Evangelist

For Reflection

Constitutions:
    Part VIII, [655-676], pp. 316-328
Complementary Norms: #311-320,
    pp. 317-321

Our Way of Proceeding
Week XIV

Since our communities are apostolic, they should be oriented to the service of others, particularly the poor, and to cooperation with those seeking God or working for great justice in the world. For this reason, under the leadership of superiors, communities should periodically examine whether their way of living supports their apostolic mission sufficiently and encourages hospitality. They should also consider whether their style of life testifies to simplicity, justice, and poverty.

—Complementary Norms: #323

Focus

The Surprising Presence of the of the Risen Lord Jesus

Grace

God labors for me: God loves me so much, even entering into the very struggle of life. Like a potter with clay, like a mother in childbirth, or like a mighty force blowing life into dead bones, God labors to share divine life and love. God's labors are writ large in Jesus's passion and death on a cross in order to bring forth the life of the resurrection. Once more I question myself how I can make a response. Let me look again to the expression of the prayer Take and Receive.

—Spiritual Exercises #236

Questions

What aspects or experiences of community life in the Society of Jesus have been helpful and supportive for my ministry and my own personal growth?

What have been my disappointments in Jesuit community life? If I am living alone at present or have lived alone in the past, what helps me feel connected to the Society?

What can I bring to my present community which would deepen "our union of minds and hearts?"

In my Emmaus journey in the Society, when have my eyes been opened? What have been my most significant experiences of companionship in the Society?

How have I experienced the "surprising presence" of the Risen Lord?

Week 23

April 26-May 2, 1998

For Prayer

Spiritual Exercises:
 #304-305, Upper Room, Jn. 20:19-29
 #306, Sea of Galilee, Jn. 21:1-17
Complementary Norms: #321, 325-327

Celebrations

May 1: St. Joseph the Worker
 Acts 9:1-20; Jn. 6: 52-59

For Reflection

Constitutions:
 Part VIII, [677-718], pp. 330-343
Complementary Norms:
 #321-332, pp. 323-331

Our Way of Proceeding
Week XV

Since our communities are apostolic, they should be oriented to the service of others, particularly the poor, and to cooperation with those seeking God or working for great justice in the world. For this reason, under the leadership of superiors, communities should periodically examine whether their way of living supports their apostolic mission sufficiently and encourages hospitality. They should also consider whether their style of life testifies to simplicity, justice, and poverty.

—Complementary Norms: #323

Focus

Appearances of the Risen Lord Jesus

Grace

Dearest Lord, teach me to be generous. Teach me to serve Thee as Thou deservest; to give and not to count the cost; to fight and not to heed the wounds; to toil and not to seek for rest; to labor and not ask for reward, save that of knowing that I am doing Thy will.

—Prayer of St. Ignatius for Generosity

Questions

This week we celebrate Joseph the Worker. What helps me to balance work, prayer, and relaxation in my life?

Joseph accepted Mary and her reality. His relationship was grounded and purified in faith. What are my attitudes towards Jesuits whose reality, orientation and being are difficult for me to accept?

The disciples were afraid and locked the door to the Upper Room. What, if any, are my fears which block the growth of my relationships with other Jesuits in community? What do I do to guard against individualism?

Thomas doubted and struggled with trust. Jesus was direct in his response to Thomas. How have I grown in my openness and willingness to confront and be confronted? In what specific ways am I more comfortable, direct and transparent in my relationships with other Jesuits in community?

Week 24

For Prayer

Spiritual Exercises: #230-234
Constitutions: Part IX,
    The Society's Head, and the Government
    which Descends from it. [723-735]
Complementary Norms: #395, 403, 407

Celebrations

May 3: World Day of Prayer for Vocations
    Acts 13:14,43-52; Rev. 7:9,14-17
    Jn. 10:27-30

For Reflection

Constitutions:
    Part IX, [719-811], pp. 356-372, 392-398
Complementary Norms: #333-409,
    pp. 345-357, 367-369, 373-393

Our Way of Proceeding
Week XVI

Today many problems are global in nature and therefore require global solutions. Human society itself tends toward a certain unity. Hence, it is appropriate that our society, which forms one international apostolic body, should live its universal spirit more profoundly, should effectively coordinate its resources and means and strengthen its structures, either those already established or other more flexible ones which render global and regional cooperation easier, so that it may more efficaciously respond to these problems. —Complementary Norms: #395

Focus

Vocations to the Society
Leadership and Government in the Society

Grace

I beg for the gift of an intimate knowledge of all the sharing of goods which God does in his love for me. Filled with gratitude, I want to be empowered to respond just as totally in my love and service of him. —Spiritual Exercises: #233

Questions

As we move toward the conclusion of our Province retreat, how have I grown in my understanding and appreciation of my Jesuit vocation?

Am I reluctant or eager to suggest to a young man that he consider a Jesuit vocation if he appears to be a suitable candidate? (Ignatius wanted companions who were generous, talented, passionate and committed.)

What has been my experience of Superiors in the Society? How have I been treated by them? In turn, how have I supported them in carrying out the responsibilities the Society has given them?

How have I grown in my trust of Superiors? What has helped me grow in this trust? What helps me become more open, honest, and vulnerable with Superiors?
What characteristics do I expect and admire in Superiors? Which of these qualities do I find in myself?

If I have experienced unjust or harsh treatment from Superiors, am I now moved in prayer to forgive them as I wish, in turn, to be forgiven?

Week 25

The Society was not instituted by human means; and it is not through them that it can be preserved and increased, but through the grace of the omnipotent hand of Christ our God and Lord. Therefore in him alone must be placed the hope that he will preserve and carry forward what he deigned to begin for his service and praise and for the aid of souls. —Constitutions #812

For Prayer

Spiritual Exercises: #235-237

Constitutions: Part X,
How the Whole Body of the Society is to be Preserved and Increased in its Well-Being. [813-814], [816], [821]

Complementary Norms: #411-412

Celebrations

May 14: St. Matthias, Apostle

May 16: St. Andrew Bobola, SJ

For Reflection

Constitutions: Part X,
[812-827] pp. 400-407

Complementary Norms: #410-416
pp. 401-403

Focus

Gratitude for God's gifts; "…the Reason for our Hope"

Grace

God's gifts to me: God creates me out of love and desires nothing more than a return of love on my part. So much does God love me that even though I turn away and make little response, this Giver of all good gifts continues to be my Savior and Redeemer. All my natural abilities and gifts, along with the gifts lavished upon me, are only so many signs of how much God our Lord shares divine life with me and wants to share ever more. My consolation: who I am by the grace of God!

If I were to respond as a reasonable person, what could I give in return to such a Lover? Moved by love, I may want to express my own love-response in the following words: 'Take, Lord, and receive.'

—Spiritual Exercises #234

Questions

A very significant aspect of Ignatian spirituality is a growing capacity to find God in all things. During this week, how have I discovered the presence and action of God in my life?

As I reflect on the graces of the past weeks of this retreat, where have I noticed faithful patterns of God's action and presence?

Ignatius wanted the early Companions to constantly reflect on their experience. The *Autobiography*, *Spiritual Exercises* and the *Constitutions* are Ignatius' own reflection on his experience. For Ignatius, a key component in this daily reflection process was the *Examen*. What do I find helpful when using this simple, effective prayer which heightens awareness of God's presence and action?

Since one of the main purposes of this retreat is to lead us to a growing awareness and freedom for communal discernment, what am I discovering through my experience of these weekly spiritual conversations?

Our Way of Proceeding
Week XVII

Week 26

For Prayer

Spiritual Exercises:
    #312 Ascension, Acts 1:1-12
    #307 Mission to the World, Mt. 28:16-20
GC 34, Decree 11:
    On Having a Proper Attitude of Service
    in the Church #301, 313

Celebrations

May 21: The Ascension of the Lord Jesus
    Acts 1:1-11; Eph. 1:17-23
    or Heb. 9:24-28,10:19-23;
    Lk. 24:46-53

For Reflection

C 34, Decree 11:
    On Having a Proper Attitude of Service
    in the Church

…Ignatian service in the Church is not a history lesson. It is a profound mystical bond that transcends the particularities of it historical origins in the sixteenth-century church.
        —GC 34, Decree 11: A Proper Attitude of Service in the Church #313

Our Jesuit service can also be the dangerous commitment of witness and struggle against the forces of injustice and persecution, both social and religious, a witness that has been once again sealed by the blood of martyrs. In recent decades, as throughout our history, the heroism of our many brothers who have suffered and died for their fidelity to the Church bears clear and irrefutable witness that the Society's foundational commitment is truly 'to serve the Lord alone and the Church, his spouse, under the Roman Pontiff.
        —GC 34, Decree 11: On Having a Proper Attitude of Service in the Church #301

Focus

Ascension of the Lord Jesus: His Mission to the World

Grace

…men crucified to the world, and to whom the world itself is crucified—such would our Constitutions have us to be; new men, I say, who have…put on Christ; dead to themselves to live to justice; who…in labors, watchings…in chastity, in knowledge, in long-suffering…in charity unfeigned, in the word of truth, show themselves ministers of God; and by the armor of justice…by honor and dishonor, by evil report and good report, by good success finally and ill success, press forward with great strides….This is the sum and aim of our institute.
        —Pedro de Ribadeneria, SJ, Preface to the First Edition of the Constitutions

Questions

GC 34 labored to craft this document into a contemporary expression of the "Rules for thinking with the Church." What was my reaction as I read and pondered this decree?

Authority: What is my present attitude toward those holding authority in the Church: the Pope and the Hierarchy? What is my attitude toward authority in the Society of Jesus?

Service: *Hunger, religious and racial persecution, disordered economic and cultural development, the lack of political freedom and social justice; the widespread socio-economic discrimination, exploitation, and sexual abuse, especially of women and children; the callous disregard for the precious gift of life; the pastoral challenges of secularity, the social anonymity and alienation of modern urbanization, the dissolution of the family—all these confront, often massively, the Church and therefore ourselves, and demand our response.*
        —GC 34, Decree 11: On Having a Proper Attitude of Service in the Church #307

What has been my personal response to these issues?

What do I hope we, as a Province, will do to address these issues?

Week 27

May 24-31, 1998

For Prayer

Spiritual Exercises: #233

GC 34, Decree 26:
 Characteristics of Our Way of Proceeding
 #539

Celebrations

May 30: Vigil of Pentecost
 Acts 28:16-20,30-31; Jn. 21:20-25
 Veni Creator
May 31: Pentecost
 Acts 2:1-11; 1 Cor.12:3-7,12-13
 Jn. 20:19-23 or Acts 2:1-11; Rom.8:8-17
 Jn. 14:15-16,23-26

For Reflection

GC 34, Decree 26:
 Characteristics of our Way of Proceeding

Today we bring this counter cultural gift of Christ to a world beguiled by self-centered human fulfillment, extravagance, and soft living, a world that prizes prestige, power, and self-sufficiency. In such a world, to preach Christ poor and humble with fidelity and courage is to expect humiliation, persecution, and even death. We have seen this happen to our brothers in recent years. Yet we move forward resolutely out of our "desire to resemble and imitate in some manner our creator and Lord Jesus Christ... since He is the way which leads men to life." Today, as always, it is deep, personal devotion to Jesus, himself the Way, that principally characterizes the Jesuit way of proceeding. —GC 34, Decree 26: Characteristics of Our Way of Proceeding #539

I beg for the gift of an intimate knowledge of all the goods which God lovingly shares with me. Filled with gratitude, I want to be empowered to respond just as totally in my love and service.
—Spiritual Exercises: #233

Focus

Review the Graces of this Retreat

Grace

Take, Lord, and receive all my liberty, my memory, my understanding, and my entire will—all that I have and call my own. You have given it all to me. To you, Lord, I return it. Everything is yours; do with it what you will. Give me only your love and your grace. That is enough for me.
—Spiritual Exercises: #234

Questions

What aspect, component or characteristic of "Our Way of Proceeding" gives me strength, hope and energy both for the present and for our future together?

"The major work of GC 34 has been the revision of our law and the orientation of our mission for today." What has been my experience during this retreat of reflecting with other Jesuits on the Constitutions and documents of GC 34?

How would I describe my openness and freedom to enter Province deliberations and decisions affecting the direction of our ministries in the future?

As we prepare to conclude our Province retreat on the feast of Pentecost, how do I perceive the Holy Spirit to be active and present in my life and in the life of the Society of Jesus?
How have I been moved by the power of God's presence, action, and grace in this retreat?

Ignatius the pilgrim has been our companion on this retreat. Do I experience renewed desire to journey in faith with other companions as we move with hope into the future on our "pathway to God?"

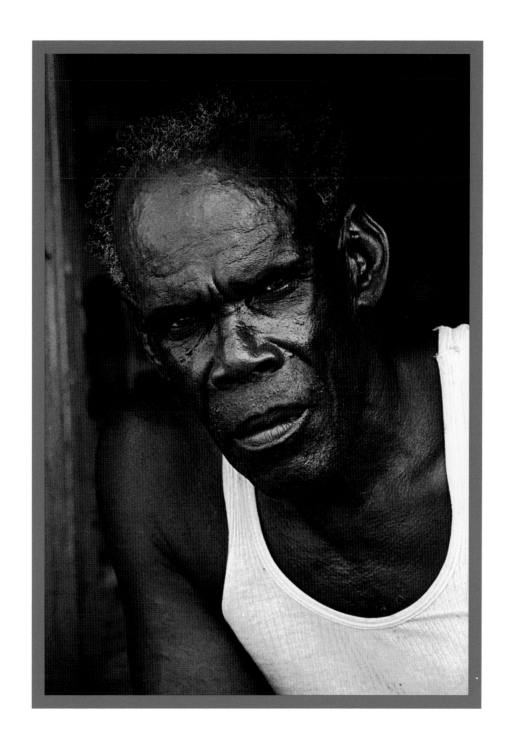

The Photographs

Week 16 (*page 40*)
    Omaha, NE, 1996, Jim Michalski at the Jesuit Middle School
Week 17 (*page 42*)
    Omaha, NE, 1997, Homecare for the sick
Week 18 (*page 44*)
    Jerusalem, 1984, Praying at the Wall
Week 19 (*page 46*)
    Omaha, NE, 1993, Larry Helmueller anointing the sick
Week 20 (*page 48*)
    Luena, Angola, 1997, Crucified today -- landmine victim
Week 21 (*page 80*)
    Jerusalem, 1984, Boy at entrance of tomb
Week 22 (*page 48*)
    Sri Lanka, 1994, Muslim refugee on the burnt-out remains of his shelter
Week 23 (*page 80*)
    Porto Prince, Haiti 1982, Haitian woman on way to the market
Week 24 (*page 48*)
    Capernaum, Israel, 1984, Shepherd by Sea of Galilee where Jesus preached and fed 5000 people
Week 25 (*page 80*)
    Rome, Italy, 1995, Fr. Peter Hans Kolvenbach, SJ addresses the 34th General Congregation
Week 26 (*page 48*)
    San Salvador, El Salvador, 1990, First Anniversary of Jesuit Martyrs and their companions
Week 27 (*page 80*)
    Belize, 1968, Man in Orangewalk's town center

Acknowledgements

I am grateful to the many people who have helped bring this book to completion. You know who you are and you know my gratitude. I am especially appreciative of Elizabeth O'Keefe for her sensitivity and artistic skill in the final design of this book. It was a joy for me to work with her and Don Doll, SJ.